How to Draw
AQUARIUM ANIMALS

Barbara Soloff Levy

Dover Publications, Inc.
Mineola, New York

Note

The wonders of the sea include eight-legged octopuses, menacing eels, leaping dolphins, and many other fascinating creatures. This easy-to-use book will show you how to draw these and other sea animals in several steps.

Before you begin, look at the drawings on each page. You will start each drawing with a simple shape. With each step, you add more details to the picture. The last step is completing the drawing of the animal.

You may want to trace the steps for each picture first, just to get a feel for drawing. Then you can begin to make your drawing using a pencil, which is easy to erase. Follow the steps in number order.

If you are not pleased with your drawing, you can keep working at it, erasing and then drawing new lines. When you are satisfied with the results, you can go over the lines with a felt-tip pen or colored pencil. Erase the dotted lines when you get to the last step. Finally, you can color in your drawings to make your aquarium animals come to life!

Bibliographical Note

How to Draw Aquarium Animals is a new work, first published by Dover Publications, Inc., in 2003.

Library of Congress Cataloging-in-Publication Data

Soloff Levy, Barbara.
    How to draw aquarium animals / Barbara Soloff Levy.
       p. cm.
    ISBN 0-486-43058-8 (pbk.)
      1. Marine animals in art. 2. Drawing—Technique. I. Title.
    NC781.S618 2003
    743.6'7—dc21
                                       2003048973

Manufactured in the United States of America
Dover Publications, Inc., 31 East 2nd Street, Mineola, N.Y. 11501

Anemone   1

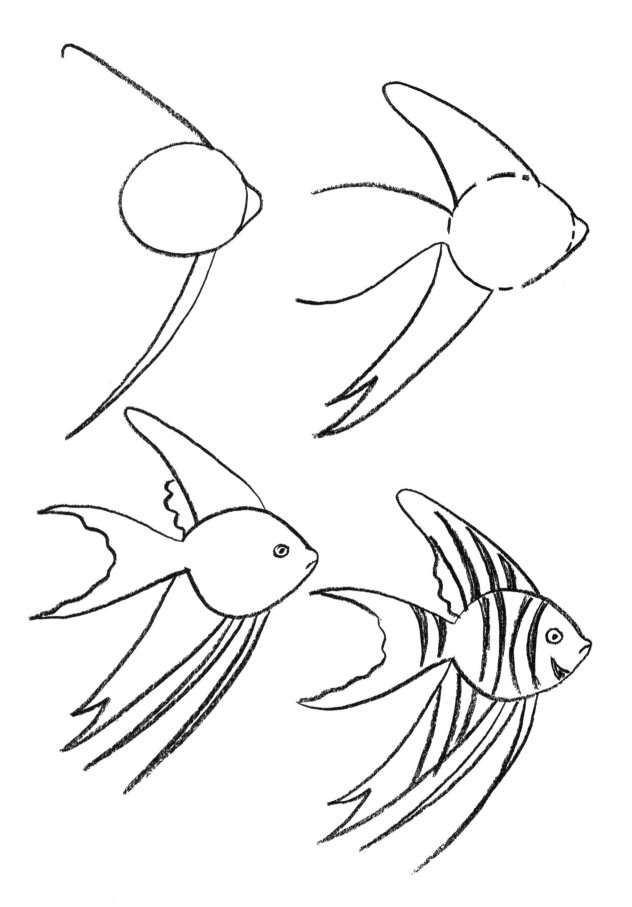

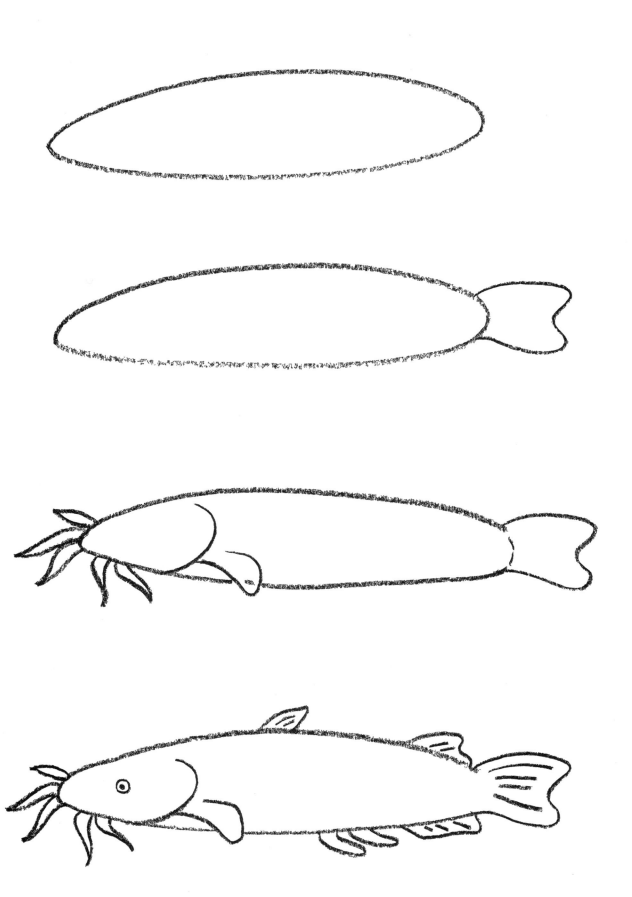

Catfish 3

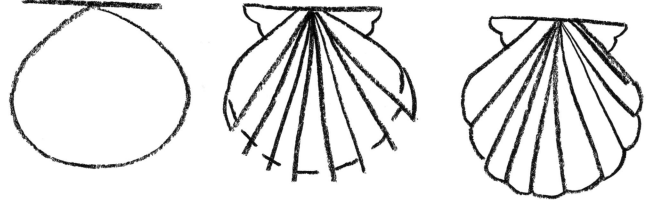

4   Clam/Scallop

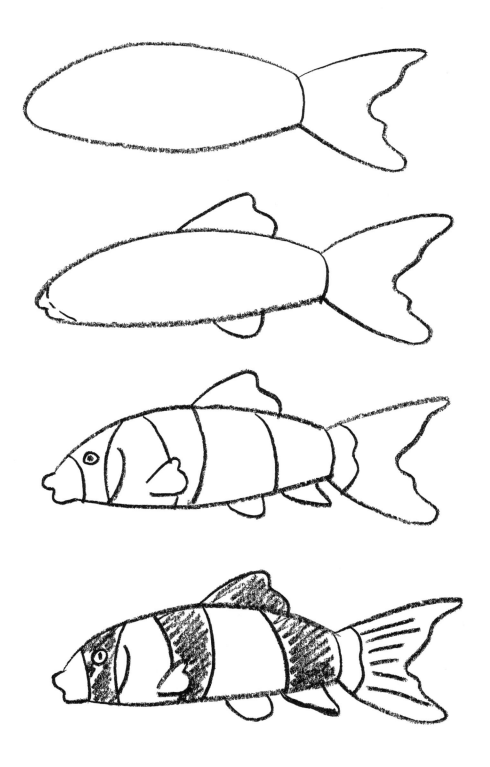

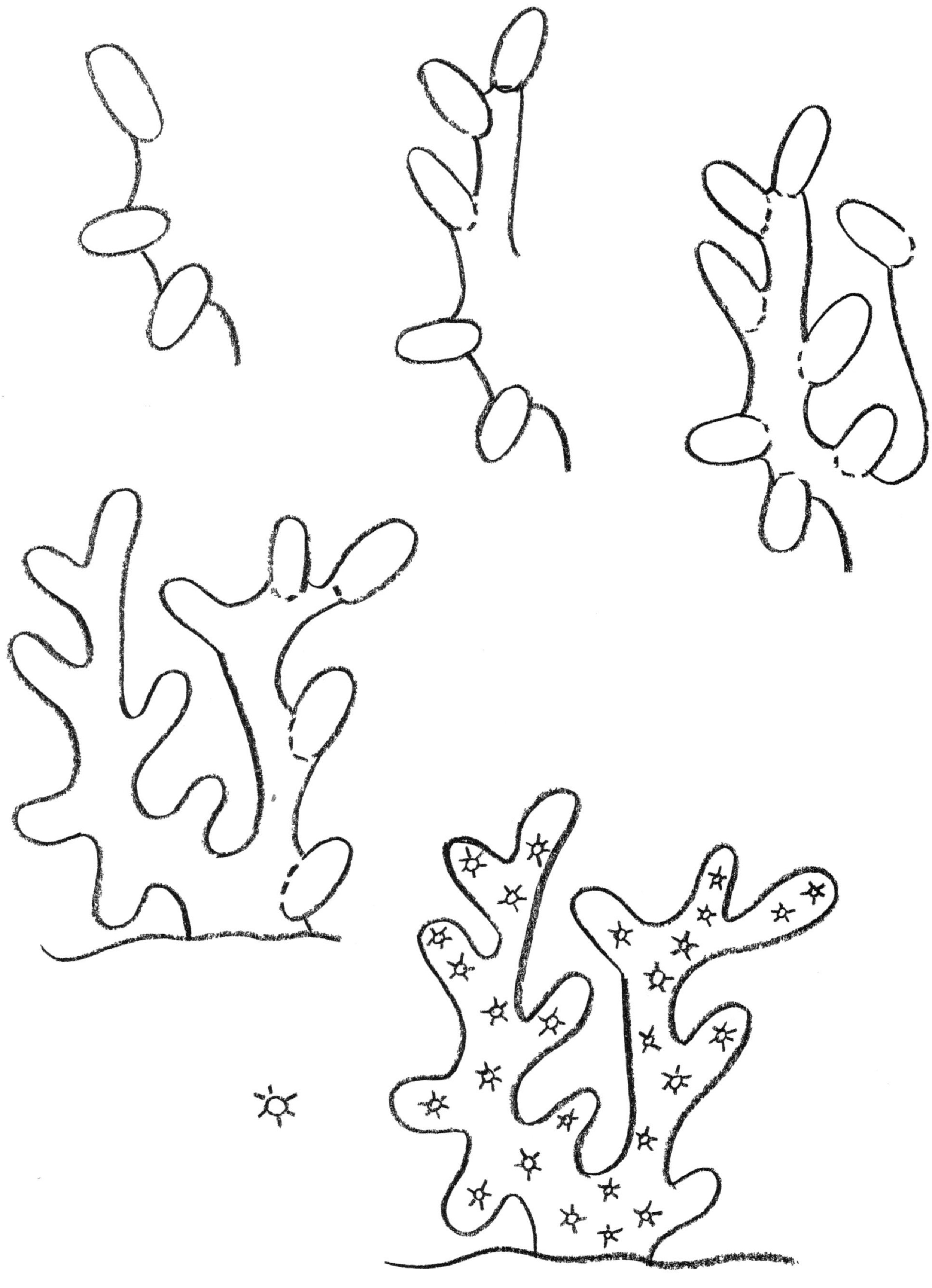

Crab 7

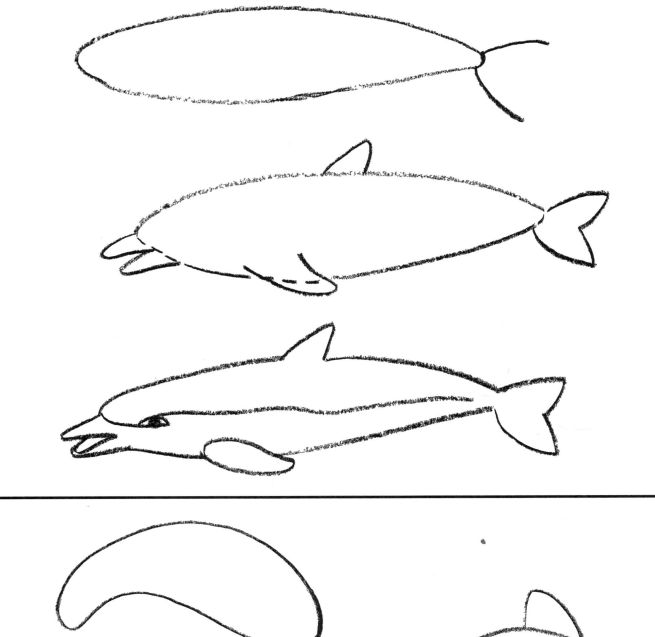

8   Dolphin

Frog 9

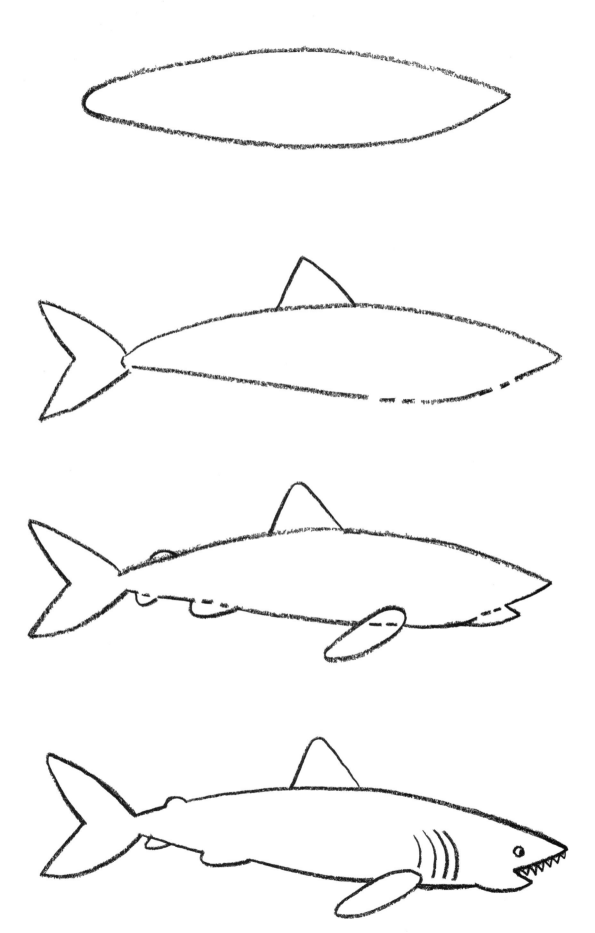

10   Great White Shark

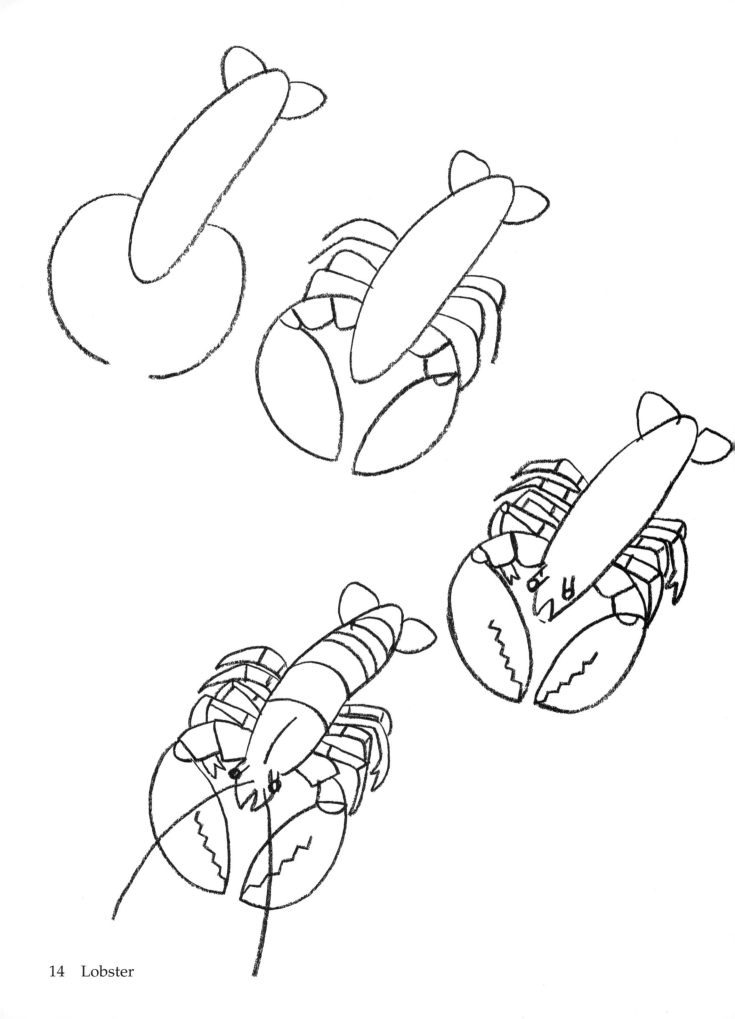

14 Lobster

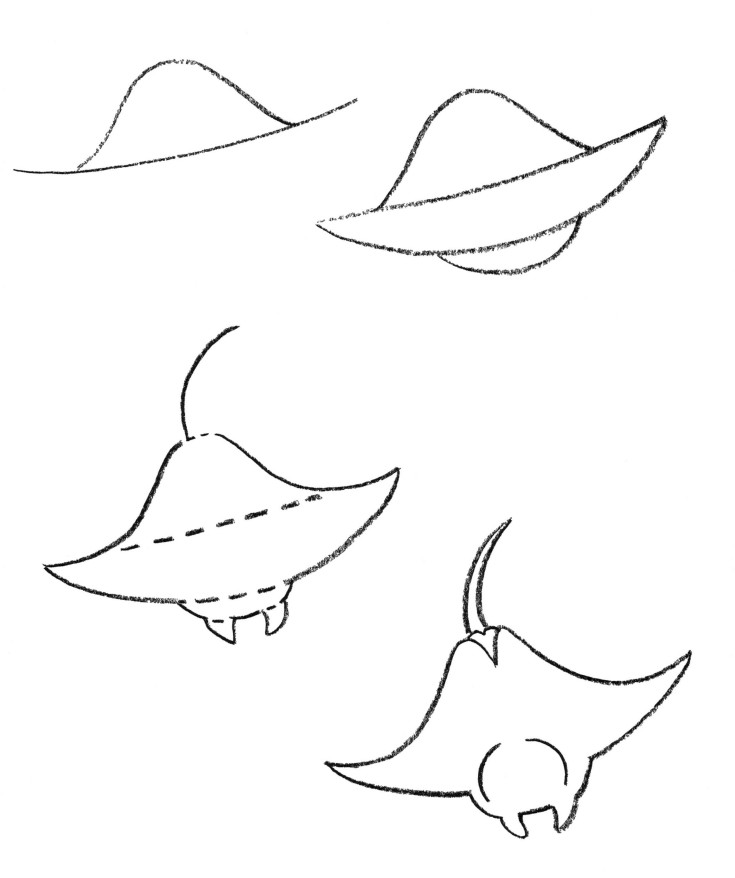

Manta Ray   15

18   Sea Horse

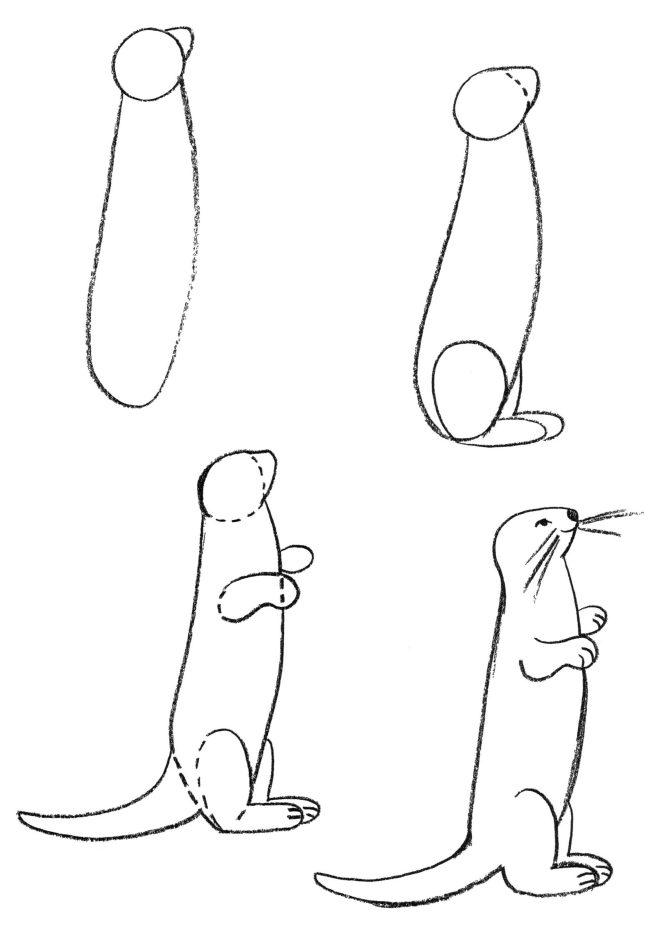

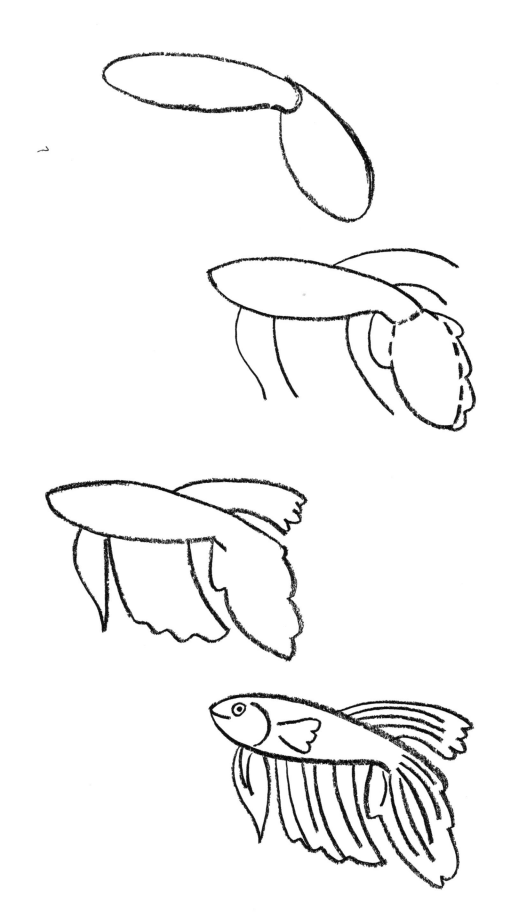

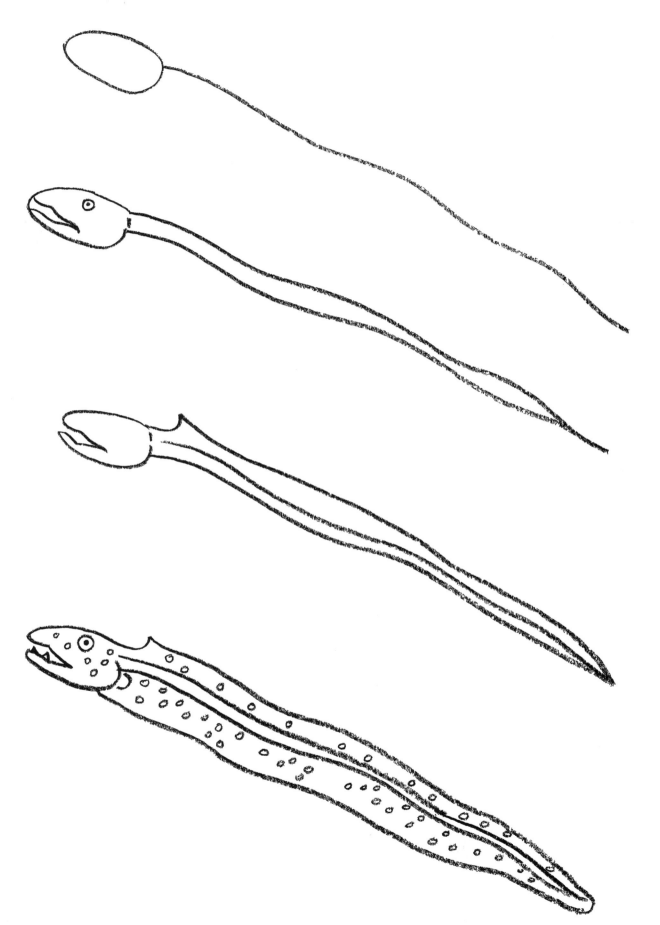

Spotted Moray Eel   25

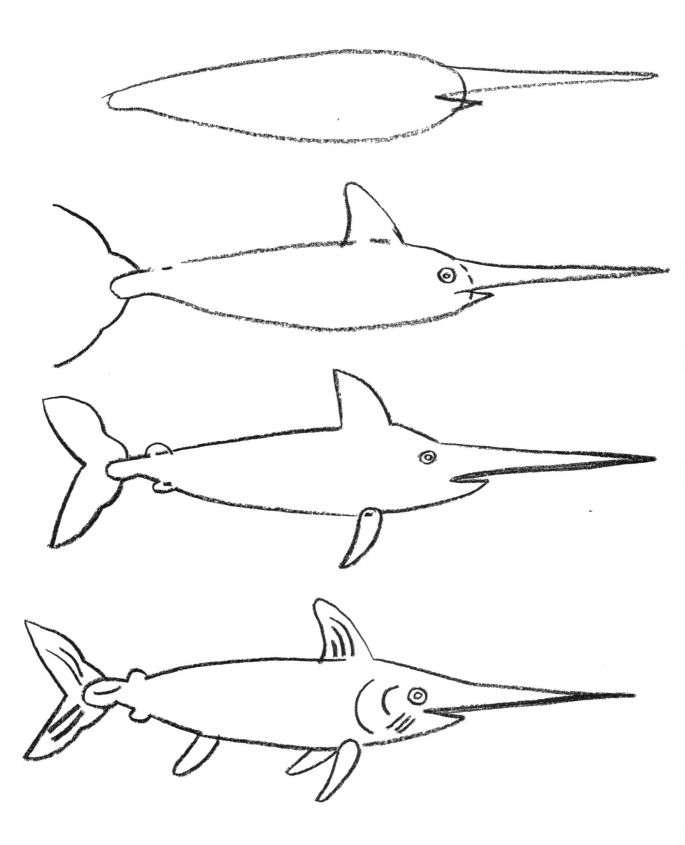

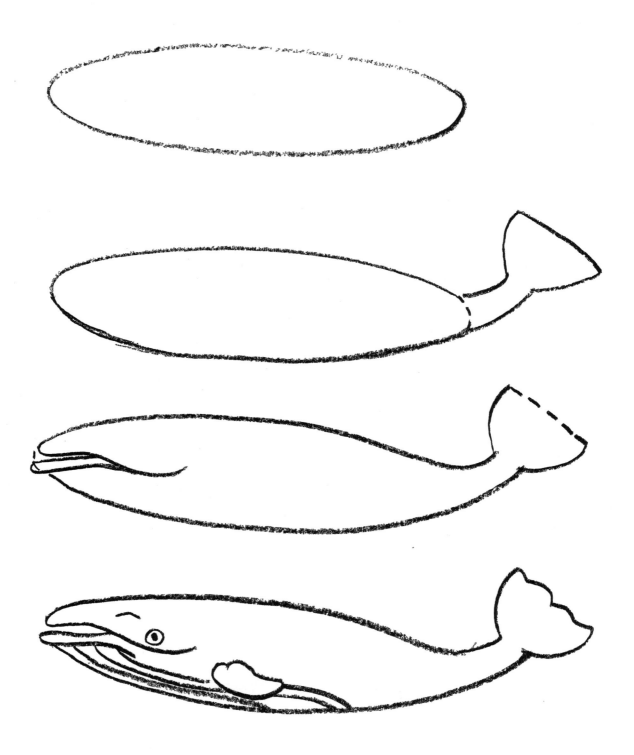